Golf Spoof and Trivia Book

By

William Kociemba

&

Eric A. Kaufman

Illustrated By

Steve Sack

Cover design by Jon Bass

Interior design by Michelle Fournier

Interior photographs courtesy of Comedy III Entertainment, Inc.

Published by Gazelle, Inc.
40940 County Center Drive
Temecula, California 92590, U.S.A.
www.golfinstuff.com

First edition
Printed in Hong Kong

ISBN 0-9667876-0-9

Thank You

Moe, Larry, Shemp, Curly, Joe and Curly-Joe
for leaving us with a legacy of laughter.

Dedication

This book is dedicated to all the "scratch" golfers out there,
especially those that scratch their heads after every other shot!

Acknowledgments

We'd like to thank the following people for their time and talents in making this book possible.

Comedy III Entertainment for providing us with photographs and informative tidbits for the trivia sections.

Steve Sack for his patience and professionalism. Nobody captures an expression better than him.

Jon Bass of Reprints, Inc. the illustrator of the Country Club scene.

The talented Michelle Fournier of The Graphic Dept. for her exceptional work in laying out this book.

O'Brian Kaufman editor-at-large, for his literary skills.

Gary Kociemba, our very special consultant and number one catalyst from early on.

To our wonderful wives Esther and Candi for their continuous support, and to the rest of our family and friends whose encouragement and insights made this project fun.

Trivia Table of Contents

"WITH ALL DA NUTS AROUND HERE YOU'D THINK HE'D LEAVE THE DANG BALL ALONE!"

THE DREAM TEAM
"TALLYiNG UP
ANOTHER "PoiFecTLY"
PLAYED HOLE

Name That Stooge™

(Trivial Stuff about the Stooges™)

1. What was Moe Howard's real name?

2. Which Stooge accidentally shot himself in the foot with a .22 rifle?

3. Which Stooge impersonated a girl in an all-girl diving act?

4. Which one of the Stooges had an obsession for dogs?

5. What was Shemp Howard's real name?

6. In addition to Larry, which of the Stooges had curly hair as a child?

7. Which musical instrument did Larry play and why?

8. Which Stooge drove a car only once in his entire life time?

9. Which Stooge had the most phobias?

10. How did Moe acquire his unique bowl-type haircut?

11. What was Larry's real name?

12. Which Stooge trained to be a boxer?

13. Which of the Stooges was an accomplished ballroom dancer?

14. Which of the Stooges had the best singing voice?

15. Did Shemp play the role of the third Stooge before or after Curly?

16. Which Stooge enjoyed hosting parties for the rich and famous?

17. Which Stooge appeared in silent movies at the age of 12?

18. Which Stooge would say "woob woob woob"?

19. Which Stooge married four times and fathered two children from different marriages?

20. Did the Three Stooges ever appear in a film with Laurel & Hardy?

Answers To Trivia Questions

1. His given name was Harry Moses Horwitz. In school he was known as Moe, a name that would later become legendary in show business.

2. Curly. Accidents can happen and soitenly happened in his career. (See *Occupational Hazards of Being a Stooge* section.)

3. Moe. He wore a one-piece bathing suit with paper falsies for breasts when he toured with the *Annette Kellerman's Diving Girls*. After each dive, he would have to stay under water until he pushed the paper falsies back into place.

4. Curly. In the early vaudeville days, he would buy a dog in nearly every city that the Stooges played. He would keep it with him for about a week and then ship it home to Los Angeles.

5. Samuel Horwitz. His Hebrew name was Schmool which was Anglicized to Samuel or Sam. When his mother would pronounce Sam in her broad European accent, it sounded like Shemp!

6. Moe. By the time Moe was six years old (1903), his curly hair was almost to his shoulders. Moe's mother always wanted a girl (all five of her children were boys), so Moe would please his mother by allowing her to curl his hair every morning before school. As a result, Moe was constantly teased in school for his "girly hair" and was engaged in fist fights on almost a daily basis until he was eleven.

7. The violin. When he was a small child, he burned his arm with acid and required a major skin graft. He was given a violin to play as therapy to repair the damaged nerves in his arm. Larry became an accomplished violinist, and used this talent in his early vaudeville act and Stooge™ shorts.

8. Shemp. Moe and Shemp went in as partners on their first car (a Pope Hartford that cost $90 used and had no brake linings). As part of the deal, Moe was to give Shemp driving lessons. During the lesson, Shemp let go of the steering wheel to squeeze the bulb horn with both hands. Before the horn went off, the car went through a barber shop window and stopped when it hit the barbers chair. Fortunately the shop was closed. From that day forward, Shemp never drove a car again. In films where Shemp was supposed to be driving a car, it was actually being pulled along by a stuntman.

9. Shemp. He had a fear of driving, flying, heights, water and dogs. In the movie *Hold That Lion*, Shemp had to do a scene with an old sickly lion. Shemp was so frightened, that technicians had to put a glass plate between Shemp and the lion.

10. After years of being teased and bullied about his ten inch long curls, Moe took a pair of scissors and circled his head clipping off all of his curls. The result was a bowl shaped haircut.

11. Louis Fineburg.

12. Larry, a man who could deliver or receive a punch with the best of them.

13. Curly. He was a graceful dancer that frequented night clubs. Remember the Curly shuffle?

14. Curly. He had a beautiful tenor voice.

15. Shemp actually was a Stooge along with his brother Moe before Larry joined the act. During the vaudeville and early movie years with Ted Healy (the original act was Ted Healy and his Stooges), the Stooges were Moe, Larry and Shemp. After disputes with Ted Healy, Shemp decided to leave the act and pursue what became a successful acting career. After Curly's first stroke in 1946, Shemp rejoined the Stooges in his younger brother's place. Shemp remained with the team until his death in 1955.

16. Larry. It's rumored that he also enjoyed putting silverware in his pockets at other parties.

17. Moe. A star was born!

18. Curly. A true ladies man!

19. Curly.

20. Yes. The film entitled *Hollywood Party* (MGM 1934) featured the Stooges, Laurel & Hardy and other stars of the day.

PLAYiNG The HiGH
Lie-STOOGe STYLe

I'S COMIN' TO PLAY!

In the early years of the Stooges, they were known as Ted Healy and his Stooges. Ted Healy was a big vaudeville and film star of the period, as well as a childhood friend of Moe's. After several breakups precipitated by Ted Healy's unfair treatment of the Stooges, Moe managed to convince Ted to release the Stooges from their contract with him and MGM. Larry and Curly were concerned about their ability to go out on their own, but Moe knew that there was a place for them in films... the question was where?

TWO REELER TRIVIA

That's when they decided to call themselves The Three Stooges. On the day the Stooges left Ted Healy and the MGM studio lot, they agreed to meet later that afternoon to discuss their future plans. Moe was approached by an agent from Columbia before he even got to his car. He went down to Columbia and was given a contract to make a two-reel comedy. At the same time, an agent from Universal Studios approached Larry as he was leaving the studio, so Larry accompanied that agent to Universal to sign a contract. Later that day the Stooges discovered that they were under contract with two studios at the same time. Since the time stamped on the Columbia contract was earlier than the Universal contract, the Stooges belonged to Columbia. What began as a one-picture contract, went on to become twenty-four years of two-reel comedies (1934-1958).

Two-reelers, otherwise known as "shorts," each less than twenty minutes in length, were produced by the studio as "curtain raisers" to be shown before the feature film presentation. Studio management considered the shorts to be "throwaways," and they paid little attention to their production as long as they were completed on schedule.

Because each short had to be shot in less than a week, time was of the essence. At Columbia most of them had to be filmed in three days. The Stooges, however, were usually allowed an extra day of shooting time, primarily because of the often elaborate sight gags involved. Although the market for two-reel comedies began to fade, the demand for the Stooge shorts were very high among theatre owners. At times, Columbia forced theatre owners to take one of their "B" pictures if they wanted a Stooge two-reeler.

HAVING
A COURSE
CONNIPTION in
LIVING COLOR

LINKS AND LEGENDS

BiRD ATTeMPT on #12

The Occupational Hazards of being a Stooge™

The Stooges rarely used stunt doubles and were very adept at taking falls. However, the job description for being a Stooge meant that you were inevitably in for some bumps and bruises. Here is a list of some trivial and not so trivial injuries suffered by the boys during their careers as Stooges:

In their first short with Columbia *(Women Haters, 1934)*, Larry broke his finger while tumbling out of a sleeping berth during a scene in a Pullman car.

In their second film, *(Punch Drunks, 1934)* Curly played a prize fighter who would go crazy when Larry played *Pop Goes the Weasel* on his violin. Curly suffered a bloody nose and a cut lip while playing a scene in the ring with a professional boxer.

In the film *Men In Black*, 1934, the Stooges were cut by flying glass when they slammed a glass door in one of the hospital scenes.

For their first football film, *Three Little Pigskins* (1934), the football scenes were shot with football players from Loyola University. According to Moe, "they knew how to tackle and they tackled hard." During the touchdown run scene, Moe, Larry and Curly were supposed to stop for news photographers on the sideline where they are pounced on by the entire Loyola football team. When the Stooges reviewed this scene they saw trouble with an entire team of two-hundred-pounders pouncing on top of them. The Stooges informed the director that they wanted stunt doubles to do this scene. They never used stunt doubles before, but they knew that they needed them now. The director, Raymond McCarey said, "Listen, fellows, you know how to take falls. You've done enough of them. It will take hours to find doubles for you. Besides we can't afford them. Don't worry, you won't get hurt." But the Stooges still refused to do the scene and within an hour stunt doubles were on the field ready for the scene. During the scene, all of the players, including the doubles, landed in a heap on top of the newsmen. As the heap unraveled, two of the stunt doubles had broken legs, all four newsmen had either broken arms or legs and all of them wound up in the hospital except for Curly's stunt double. Apparently, he was padded all over to resemble Curly and the padding broke the blows.

During a scene in *Ants in the Pantry* (1936), the Stooges played exterminators. Since they were having trouble selling their services, their boss said, "If they don't have bugs, then give them some." So the Stooges went from house to house throwing mice on the floor and ants in the pantry. In one scene, Moe hadn't noticed that a container of red ants had broken in his pocket and they were crawling down his back, in his hair and into his pants. Throughout the scene, Moe was scratching, squirming, and slapping himself on the neck and the seat of his pants. The elated director screamed, "Great Moe. Keep up that squirming."

In the film, *Hoi Polloi* (1935), a scene called for the leading lady, Grace Goodall, to laugh loudly with her mouth wide open while Moe hit her in the face with a cream puff. Moe, who was a perfect shot due to his childhood experience with pea shooters and spitballs, hit Grace squarely in the mouth with the cream puff. However, it lodged so deeply down her throat that some of the cream had gone down her windpipe and she grasped for breath. There were some moments of concern, but they finally brought her around.

More than 150 pies were thrown during the 16 minute comedy *Slippery Silks* (1936). An emergency arose when they ran out of pies. The property man came onto the set and swept up all of the whipped cream he could collect from the floor to make a new batch of pies. Inside the dirty whipped cream were dust, nails and splinters. Fortunately, nobody was injured when they were hit in the face with pies full of nails. The show must go on!

Although Moe played the toughest character of the Stooges and always seemed to dish out more of the punishment than he received, he was hurt more often than Larry or Curly. Moe landed in the hospital after a scene in *Beer and Pretzels* in 1933. Moe was standing on a table that Curly was cutting with a circular saw. When the table broke, Moe was suppose to break his fall but the side of his body hit the upright legs of the table. He spoke the remainder of his lines and then passed out. Later, he learned that he had three broken ribs.

In a film where the boys were playing women wearing high-heeled shoes, Moe was skipping and one heel turned under him. In order to avoid ruining the shot, Moe slid to the side and dove into another room where he hit his head on the leg of a bed that knocked him out cold. The next day he was on crutches with a broken ankle.

Curly cut his scalp one day during a stunt where he was supposed to be dropped down an elevator shaft. The shaft was a hole large enough for Curly to disappear off camera. The floor of the hole was padded with a mattress, but the property guys neglected to cover a nearby two by four. When Curly was pushed into the hole, he cut his head on the two by four. The studio doctor clipped the hair around the wound, cleaned it and then proceeded to glue fresh hair onto the bald spot. Curly then continued on with the scene.

Larry had his share of accidents as well. He was hit in the eye with plaster, had a tooth knocked out and was even stabbed in the forehead with a quill pen.

Yes, the occupation of being a

STOOGE™

was a hazardous one!

A.A.M.
AMALGAMATED ASSOCIATION
OF MORONS LOCAL 6 7/8

Entrance Exam

The Amalgamated Association of Morons Local 6 7/8 requires all candidates to take this entrance exam to determine eligibility in joining this elite organization. The test will evaluate your background on hodgepodge, medical science, history, foreign language, and "Stooge English." Please answer the following questions with a No. 3 1/2 pencil. Cheating on this exam will result in a poke in the eyes. Please begin this exam at the sound of the cuckoo bird.

Good luck!

1. What is the Amalgamated Association of Morons Local 6 7/8?

  Ⓐ A labor union that provides protection for pie throwing.

  Ⓑ A men's only club located in the Country of Moronica where Curly does the Curly shuffle in drag.

  Ⓒ A union representing the "fruit cake" industry.

  Ⓓ The offshore corporation that the Stooges used to shelter money from the I.R.S.

  Ⓔ The national affiliate of the Mensa Organization.

2. In 1922, Ted Healy and Moe were in an act together. Ted Healy was earning $3,500 per week. What was Moe earning?

(A) The same. (B) Approximately $5,000 (C) $100 (D) Two cents.
(E) A buck three eighty.

3. Curly's mother Jennie was a:

(A) Actress. (B) Teacher. (C) Successful Real Estate agent.
(D) Mental Health evaluator. (E) Social worker.

4. If Moe was considered the first Stooge and Larry the second, how many third Stooges were there?

(A) two (B) three (C) four (D) five

5. How many shorts and feature films did the Stooges make after they went out on their own and became the Three Stooges™?

(A) 190 shorts, 6 features. (B) 71 shorts, 12 features. (C) 241 shorts, 3 features. (D) A pair of shorts that were featured in the first laundry detergent commercial.

6. Under the name The Three Stooges™, their films were made during what time period?

(A) 1910-1941 (B) 1919-1955 (C) 1934-1965
(D) Made in China a heck of a long time ago.

7. Three of these four characters were brothers; who was not?

(A) Moe (B) Curly (C) Larry (D) Shemp

8. Back in 1962, the leading attraction at the local movie theatre was?

(A) 5-cent milk duds. (B) 10-cent bottled pop.
(C) Getting the darker back row seats with your current flame.
(D) The Three Stooges shorts.

9. The oldest of the Three Stooges™ brothers was?

(A) Moe (B) Curly (C) Larry (D) Shemp

Medical

10. What names did the Stooges use when they portrayed doctors in their films?

   Ⓐ Dr. Howard, Dr. Fine, Dr. Howard
   Ⓑ Drs. Harts, Burns and Belcher
   Ⓒ Drs. Ziller, Zeller and Zoller
   Ⓓ Dr. D. Lerious, Dr. Graves and Dr. I. Yankum
   Ⓔ A, B & C

History

11. In the civil war spoof, *Uncivil Warriors*, Larry played Lieutenant Duck and Moe played Captain Dodge. What was the name of the character that Curly played in this film?

   Ⓐ General Weave Ⓑ Major Run Ⓒ Corporal Dig.
   Ⓓ Major Hyde Ⓔ Private Flee

Music Appreciation

12. What sound effect was used for the famous Three Stooges eye poke?

   Ⓐ A cuckoo clock Ⓑ Cracking a whip
   Ⓒ Whistling by famous Stooge film director Jules White
   Ⓓ A slide whistle Ⓔ The plucking of ukulele strings

Foreign Language

13. These lines were spoken in various Stooge films. *"Ver G"harget"*; *"123 Mashugana Avenue"*; *"Huck mir nisht a chynick, and I don't mean efsher!"* What foreign language, or fictional foreign language is this and what are the translations?

    (A) Yiddish. "Drop dead"; "123 Crazy Avenue"; "Don't bother me, get off my back and I don't mean maybe." (B) Moronica. "Knucklehead"; "123 Mashugana Avenue" (no translation); "Hey bunionhead, taste this (pie) and I don't mean eat it." (C) German. "Don't look now"; "123 Flower Avenue" (a type of flower found in Austria); "Hey puddinghead, take this, and I don't mean that.";
    (D) Hebrew. "Bunion brain"; "123 Nuts Avenue"; "Hey Gorilla, back into the cage and I don't mean monkey."
    (E) None of the above. The Stooges made up words in some films as part of the gags.

Stooge English

Instructions: In the following section, match the phrases to the Stooge whom so eloquently speaked 'em.

14. "I'm trying to think, but nothing happens."
    (A) Moe (B) Curly (C) Larry (D) Shemp

15. "Wake up and go to sleep."
    (A) Moe (B) Curly (C) Larry (D) Shemp

16. "You were delivered by a buzzard."
    (A) Moe (B) Curly (C) Larry (D) Shemp

17. "You told me to drop what I was doing, so I did."
    (A) Moe (B) Curly (C) Larry (D) Shemp

18. "You're a very intelligent imbecile."
    (A) Moe (B) Curly (C) Larry (D) Shemp

19. "I'm going to get myself a cheap lawyer."
    (A) Moe (B) Curly (C) Larry (D) Shemp

20. "Are you married or happy?"
    (A) Moe (B) Curly (C) Larry (D) Shemp

Answers To A.A.M. Entrance Exam

How to score you're A.A.M. Local 6 7/8 Entrance Exam:

For every correct answer give yourself five points. For every incorrect answer give yourself a big fat zero. Add your total then divide it by 7/8 (for you math morons, you can multiply your total by .875).

1. (A) A labor union that provides protection for pie throwing. From the film *Half-Wits Holiday*. Score:_____

2. (C) $100.00 – quite a bargain! Score:_____

3. (C) Jennie Horwitz was a successful real estate agent. Score:_____

4. (C) Four – Shemp, Curly, Joe Besser, Curly-Joe DeRita. Score:_____

5. (A) 190 shorts, 6 features. Score:_____

6. (C) Under the name of The Three Stooges™, films were produced from 1934-1965. Score:_____

7. (C) Moe, Shemp and Curly were brothers (Horwitz). Larry was not related. Score:_____

8. (D) Three Stooges shorts with (C) a close second. Score:_____

9. (D) The oldest of the Horwitz brothers was Shemp. Score:_____

10. (E) A, B & C. Score:_____

11. (D) Major Hyde. As in Duck, Dodge and Hyde. Score:_____

NYUK, NYUK, NYUK, NYU

12. (E) The plucking of ukulele strings was used for
    this sound effect.   Score:_____

13. (A) Yiddish. The Stooges worked some of their Jewish
    heritage into their films.   Score:_____

14. Curly   Score:_____

15. Moe   Score:_____

16. Moe   Score:_____

17. Larry   Score:_____

18. Moe   Score:_____

19. Larry   Score:_____

20. Curly   Score:_____

                                                          TOTAL:_____

Total Score multiplied by 7/8 (X .875):

Grading Curve

65.63 to 87.5
Sorry, no brain soygens admitted!

52.5 to 65.62
Hmmm… a fairly intelligent imbecile, there may be hope.

43.75 to 52.4
It's a no-brainer, you are eligible for the A.A.M. M.I.T.
(Morons In Training) Program.

43.74 and below
Congratulations, you are a true Moron!
Welcome to the A.A.M. Local 6 7/8.

This test was compiled, compelled and commingled by the prestigious accounting firm of Dewey Cheatum and Howe. Candidates that failed to qualify may still join by filing an affidavit that states under penalty of perjury that the candidate is a *half-brother to a weasel*. Please send a notarized affidavit along with a note from a veterinarian to the A.A.M. care of the Law Firm of Howard, Fine and Howard, Glendale, California, 91203.

Amalgamated Association of Morons

On this _____ day of _____, in the year _____, by order of Chief Morons of the A.A.M. and the National Counsel of Morons representing A.A.M. Local chapters, hereby, thereby and whereby certify that:

_____

Is a member in good standing of the Amalgamated Association of Morons, Local **6 7/8**. The above named inductee has achieved the status of:

☐ **True Moron**　　☐ **M.I.T** *(Moron In Training)*

Membership in this exclusive Association provides the above named to union protection for Pie Throwing, in addition and not limited to, entitling the member to unlimited Mulligans while engaged in the game of golf.

Duly signed and sealed by:

Howard, Fine & Howard

Howard, Fine & Howard　　Chief Morons, A.A.M.

ASSOCIATION OF MOROИS
AMALGAMATED
AAM
Local 6 7/8
NYUK NYUK!

The THREE STOOGES™

PHOTO

Album

Moe was the second youngest of
five boys in the Horwitz family.

Shemp enjoyed a successful acting career on his
own and as a member of The Three Stooges™

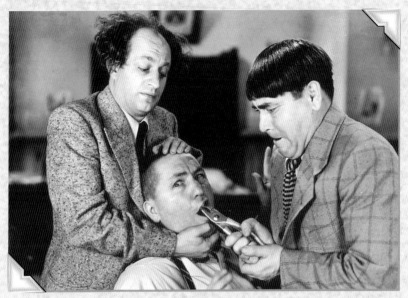

Hold still or I'll pull your gizzard out!

Happy trails.

Ready… aim… How about some fire boys?

Hey look here Moe, a note from the IR and S.

A couple of dumbells and an airbag.

Oh no! An IRS agent has arrived.

A sight for sore eyes.

We know a good dummy when we see one.
You're gonna' be a big star.

It's Showtime!

This way for a Tunis Fish sandwich.

Oops!

The big shots with some beauties.

He's the captain you Knucklehead,
not the chaplain!

The cover girls dressed to kill.

We're pleading the 4th, 5th, 6th, 7th & 8th.

Shave and a haircut - two bits.

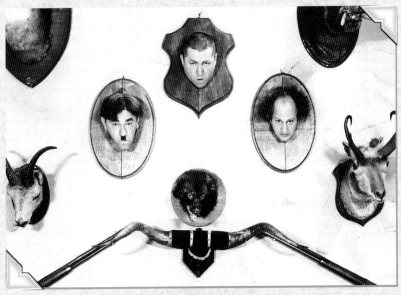

Heads of their class.

Perched partridge on a picklebrain.

Moe sings bass, Curly sings tenor,
and ole Larry joins right in…

I don't see any loose wires up here!

Mind over manners.

Bubble trouble.

It's just about Slappy Hour.

Woob… Woob… Woob…

Face it, you're just a big baboon.

I want my mummy!

The Three Little Pigskins.

The Stooges on top of their game.

We guarantee it!

Dizzy Doctors - 1937

Roll'em right here boys.

Any body home?

Prunin' a puddin' head

The good, the bad, and the chubby.

First a bannana and then a havana-
you boys are good.

Hook, line and sinker,
fresh fish and a couple of stinkers.

Bibliography

Howard, Moe. *Moe Howard & The 3 Stooges*. Secaucus, New Jersey: Carol Publishing Group, 1977.

Lenburg, Jeff, Joan Howard Mauer and Greg Lenburg. *The Three Stooges Scrapbook*. Secaucus, New Jersey: Carol Publishing Group, 1997.

Kurson, Robert. *The Official Three Stooges Encyclopedia*. Chicago, Illinois: NTC/Contemporary Publishing Group, Inc., 1998.

Additional information and photographs provided by *Comedy III Entertainment, Inc.*, Glendale, California.

SMASHING
GIFT IDEAS

- **The Holiday Season**
- **"Boithdays"**
- **Golf Enthusiasts**
- **Business Gifts**
- **Father's Day Chuckles**

- **Three Stooges™ Enthusiasts**
- **Get Well Gifts (Hospitals), etc.**
- **Business Promotions**
- **Prizes for Golf Tournaments**

105

From These Legendary Comics!

Since 1929, The Three Stooges style of humor has been enjoyed by millions. With The Three Stooges™ popularity at an all time high, these novel gift ideas would be a welcomed addition to any golf'n Stooges™ collection.

Bring Humor To The Tee-Box With Larry, Moe & Curly!

The Three Stooges™ Talking Golf Head Covers

Yes… they talk! Each character says two unique wisecracks to provide the poifect comment to your golf partners' less than perfect tee shot – a total of six unique one-liners recorded by the world's best impersonator's. Simply squeeze the left hand and let them do the talking for you… "Nice shot Knucklehead™". They fit easily on even oversized club heads.

Keep your Knuckles dry... Knucklehead™!

"Property of Three Stooges™ Country Club" Golf Towel. This towel is of exceptional quality with vivid colors and detail. Made of 100% cotton velour measuring 16"x 24" (large enough to polish Curly's bald-head). Golf towels are available separately or as part of a gift set.

Three Stooges™ Country Club Bag/Luggage Tag

Identify your golf bag or luggage with this prestigious Three Stooges™ Country Club Bag Tag. This tag clearly identifies the owner as a member of this exclusive Country Club and an official Golf'n Stooge™.

Country Club Divot Tool

Designed to repair Stooges™ size divots. After all, they were the experts when it came to divots! This heavy metal tool is engraved and embossed with the Country Club Logo featuring a quality antique finish.

It's for Soiten!

The Three Stooges™ golf gift ideas would be an excellent gift for family and friends playing with slightly less than a full deck. **Nyuk! Nyuk! Nyuk!**

The Country Club Gift Set includes the Golf Towel, Bag Tag, Divot Tool, 6 golf tees and a deck of The Three Stooges™ Playing Cards packaged together in an attractive gift box.

Three Stooges™
Playing Card Gift Sets

This classic and decorative tin comes with **two decks** of hilarious Three Stooges™ Golf Cartoons in full color. A great gift idea for any Golf'n Stooge playing with slightly less than a full deck.

NYUK! NYUK! NYUK!

It's for Soiten!

Since the "Masters of Mishaps" went at it again in this enjoyable deck of 52 different playing cards, cards games have **never** been more fun.

Numbered Limited Edition Tin From The Three Stooges™ Country Club

Limited Edition

A Certificate of Authenticity is included in each tin.

This limited edition tin is adorned with the embossed The Three Stooges™ Country Club logo on the cover. Affixed to the under-side of the lid is a label identifying the tin as "Property of The Three Stooges™ Country Club" along with the tin's serial number. The tin also includes two decks of The Three Stooges™ Playing Cards, along with a fun and informational Three Stooges™ Trivia book. One trivia section includes the entrance exam to join the prestigious *A.A.M. (Amalgamated Association of Morons) Local 6 7/8*. This exam will quickly determine if you're a "Wise Guy" or a true Moron. ***Good Luck!***

Golf Tournament Prize Offer

Lighten up your golf tournament by giving the Three Stooges™ golf gift sets as prizes for: Longest putt, closest to the pin (par 3's), farthest drive, worst drive, or even host your own Three Stooges™ golf tournament. These gifts are fun, they're useful, and they're poifect!

Also available, The Three Stooges™ Country Club Golf Playing Cards, featuring 52 different and hilarious golf cartoons in full color. It's the perfect complimentary entry gift for tournament players and volunteers.

Be a "wise guy" by asking about our Three Stooges™ tournament prize package discount today.

Back of Card

Gazelle, Incorporated
40940 County Center Drive
Temecula, California 92590, U.S.A.

Phone: 888-442-0355 • Fax: 619-679-4575
www.golfinstuff.com • E-mail: golfguys@golfinstuff.com

111